If Anyone Can Hide it, it's Me.

A collection of poetry by Matthew Stegman
Cover & Illustrations by Hal Gre

Contents

Introduction……………………….... 3
Act I……………………………….. 7
Act II……………………………… 44
Act III……………………………. 81
Act IV……………………………. 130
About The Author………………..171

If Anyone Can Hide It, It's Me

The Introduction to The Introduction

Regarding art, music, or in my case writing, the creator at some point will grow beyond what they have expressed. Talking to my friend Andrea, she explains **"I only love what I aim to express or create when it's still in my head. By the time it exists on paper, or in a song, or somewhere out in the world, it's so flawed."**

I found this quite interesting, as I also in the moment of completion, hate my writing as well. Any narrative, poem, or crazed monologue written down for the sake of me staying sane, the second it managed to escape my head, I began to criticize it. Over time even began to despise it. This got me thinking as to why. Why does this happen? After talking more about her music and art, a sort of answer found its way to me.

I say to her **"I think the reason why most people hate their previous work is simply because they changed and the art, or writing, or song stayed the same."**

The reason I am giving you this introduction to the introduction, is simply because I have changed. I have changed to the point that parts of me do not want this book to be seen. Don't get me wrong I am ecstatic for it, but a lot of who I was that wrote the majority of this does not exist. I have been struggling through thoughts of not wanting to publish this because it is no longer me, but a former me. Even so, I realize now that this is a good thing. It shows my growth, it shows that I have not stayed in the same mindset as when this was written. This book represents former parts of myself I have released.

So, enjoy this version of myself as I continue to grow.

If Anyone Can Hide It, It's Me

Introduction

It's always been who I am to make a big deal out of things. Someone hurt me and I've got a body full of emotions that I never learned how to process correctly. However, I've been given enough time to think things over. Now I kind of feel like an idiot. I feel like I wasted so much time wounded and howling. Everything that meant so much is now insignificant. It doesn't matter that I took it so hard, it was just a relationship ending. It was just me reacting. How I felt had more to do with me than anything else. All this book is made up of is how I felt in moments. Poems written down when it's all I could do. So yes, I made a big deal about it. She and the relationship were a big deal. Towering over the insignificance of everything else in my life. It wasn't the first or only time I got hurt, but you just kind of forget the last time you overcame the absence of someone when it happens again. I let all my feelings burst when she left. It is so far from reality now to think of how I was. Nothing made sense for so long. We're all so complex. This book is me attempting to find some relief.

In my poetry I talk to myself, to you, and people who were personally involved. I'll give you as much context as I can. I've broken everything up into four sections. Four sections that I think convey how things progressed for me. I wanted to categorize all of my emotions and the things that took place. I wanted to line up my ducks and put them on parade. They're still quacking all the time. From when it was fresh and I was still pining for her, from me being furious about everything I'd been put through. Then to me reaching for any substance, moments

If Anyone Can Hide It, It's Me

even questioning my whole reality and myself as a person. Finally, just acceptance and understanding that it's all been a part of me growing and changing. I had to face the fact that I've been running away from how I felt. I had to learn that it's always been me hiding. It's how I've always been. I put her in place of all the issues I should have dealt with. She was the easy comfort I ran to in hope that all the things that traumatized me would go away. It was foolish to think that any person can do that for you. I still get a little crazy trying to recover, but it never lasts too long. I still lose all energy in the battle to stay positive and not let negativity overtake me. I'm feeling as good as I can these days. Which has been pretty good!

Everything that has happened and everything that I have done has left multiple dents in me. All banged up, I couldn't be happier with who I am and what I've learned. I wanted to change completely. All along this was the goal, to let myself change for the better. After everything fell apart, my plan was self-destruction. My plan was to let go and see where I ended up. I drifted a lot through it all until I found what I wanted to do.

For as long as I can remember I never wanted anything. I stayed in a constant apathy towards my life. Nothing mattered to me. I just went through the phases, not really paying attention. Probably due to traumatic events during formative years in my childhood I clammed up. Hiding in a shell protecting myself. Instead of focusing on me I always held onto any distractions or relationships. I was putting as much as I could into them and not me. This was a pattern I would continue to repeat. Over the past couple of years, I've become more aware of the pattern and aim to become better at stopping it.

It took what felt like the world ending to force me to feel something. I tried so hard to live in the world I had created

If Anyone Can Hide It, It's Me

around her. She seemed worth it, but that's because it had more to do with how I looked at myself. So, I focused on her and nothing else. She was the biggest part of my life which is sad and embarrassing. Anything can be sad and embarrassing if you stare long enough at it.

It feels silly now, thinking back to how I acted; drinking more than I could handle, spending too much time crying out for her and us. Indulging in all the bad coping mechanisms and exclaiming to the universe that I would be fine. Exclaiming that I am better off (which I am). Though, no matter how terrible I felt it was just three years. Three years of being with someone that I loved more than myself. Where even when it started to become obvious it wouldn't work, for some reason, we kept trying to make it. It was only someone leaving. Which is completely okay. It was only something that happens to everyone. What happened next was all me. It was how much of my life was built around her and everything else crashing down in her absence.

This book, and many other inadvisable choices were my therapy. It's made of sobbing and alienating myself from all of my friends. It's made of intoxication daily and embarrassing myself in front of everyone I know. Fits of anger from everything I found out after being hurt. It is a floor to ceiling window into my head and moments of self-induced insanity. It's made up of self-analysis and acceptance of the lessons I learned. We are all just stupid kids no matter how old we get. As a kid I broke everything I got my hands on. As a kid I never knew how to love or love myself. I'm still a kid going through a learning experience. Being human is a constant process. We never stop growing. I understand now that no matter how much I write her out a part of her will remain. She and what has happened is a part of me now. Everything that's me I try to write out is still going to

If Anyone Can Hide It, It's Me

be there. You're made up of everything you've ever done or said and what's been done or said to you. How we grow from that is on us. How I grew was on me.

    I understand that it is futile to run from this feeling that has clung to me for so long. This veil of depression that finds its way into all the things I do. I must face it and do everything I can to grow, just like you do. This is what I wanted to do for myself. What started as intention to get my emotions about my failed relationship out had become a period of self-reflection. You have to stare really hard in the mirror sometimes until your reflection blinks! It became more about me and what I needed to do for myself. I had to learn my self-worth and decide to be better. I couldn't keep comparing everything to what we had. Especially if it wasn't even that good. You're always given the choice to be better. I'm trying to heal now and confront everything I've been spending years ignoring. I'm still everything I was before. I thought I was so much less than I am but really, I am so much better without her. This book is me overcoming her leaving and myself. This book is a collection of poems from the end of my 'world' to the rebuilding and redefining of it.

If Anyone Can Hide It, It's Me

Act I

You left but you're still here.
In everything around me,
making a nest,
and I can't stop it.
Dammit.

If Anyone Can Hide It, It's Me

More or Less?

When they ask about you,
or how I've been,
I say, **"More or less, or maybe more of the less?"**
Because you've only given me less and less.

And I've heard you talking,
I'm as bad as you say.

I've been awake for days,
everything you've said has blurred together.
It feels like the more is less.
It feels like I have been less.

And I have,
I will continue to be.

Slow and Then All at Once

I just wanted you to touch me again,
I haven't felt anything in so long.
Our bodies resembled an ocean,
then a lake,
then a puddle.

It dried up so quickly.
We dried up so quickly.

Every bit of water in the world is gone,
including what was left in my body.

Sleeping (Mostly) Alone

There's blood in my mouth,
I've tasted it all day.
Grinding my teeth at the thought of you.
I realize now why my jaw hurts when I wake up.
Why I sleep on one side and not the other.

I'm hoping,
things will change.
I'm hoping,
to wake up and not expect you to be there.

If Anyone Can Hide It, It's Me

Mattress

I still look for you in my sleep.

It's what keeps me so drained in the morning,
and why I don't have the energy for the day.
I'm irritable and the bags under my eyes are holding all my spite.

I'm going to have to throw this mattress away,
salt and burn it.

It has all our ghosts in it.

If Anyone Can Hide It, It's Me

Does he? Does he?

When he touches you does it feel like a lover?
Are you set ablaze?
What did it feel like when I grazed against you?
Was it too rough?
Did it feel cold on your skin?
I've felt so pitiful pining for you to let me in.

He didn't even have to ask.

If Anyone Can Hide It, It's Me

Wired Wrong

Connecting has been hard,
I imagine the conversations and body language.
A tone of voice I keep up.

I feel like I can't be honest with people,
I'll just come off as crazy,
and it's not like anyone is honest with me.

I want to easily slip into someone and be welcomed.
I don't want misunderstandings.
Every situation I try and feel uncomfortable.

It was so simple,
so easy to be around you.
Who changed that?
Who changed?

The only part of me that could feel at ease,
is still inside of you.

If Anyone Can Hide It, It's Me

Autumn

If I could compare you to leaves,
I am where your tree grows.
But not where your tree wants to be.

My stability is at question,
everyone keeps asking.
But I'm not as easy as a *'yes or no'*.

I wish I was somewhere you'd change.
Green to orange to red and grays.
But where I am physically and metaphorically,
it doesn't seem like the leaves are going to fall.
Doesn't seem like your mind is going to change.

They'll never touch me.

If Anyone Can Hide It, It's Me

Open Water

Every second something's submerged.
A saltwater fish or my saltwater thoughts.
It's murky,
making things hard to process.

I don't know what made me think I could float.
I don't know what made me think I could rely on you.

I know I'll sink into the sea,
foam covering my eyes and fish biting.
I used to look for your ship.

Now it's just open water.

If Anyone Can Hide It, It's Me

Enough? Not Enough

Nothing adds up to me lately,
I just can't grasp the past,
or how to get over it.

I can't step out of this hole I dug,
with everything I've seen,
and done.
I can't stop looking behind me.

I can't.

Coffee

I've made two pots of coffee,
and managed to drink both of them.
This is recurring every other morning.
Each cup dared to whisper your name into my mouth,
as I gulped it down.

I haven't been able to keep my eyes open,
no matter how much I've drank.

Black and bitter,
no artificial sweetener could make this better.
Strangely the taste is a reminder,
of how bitter you were.
No sugar.

I'll drink two more pots,
before I let myself sleep and dream of you.

If Anyone Can Hide It, It's Me

Beach Tan

I figured I just had more time to spend,
but it's slipping.
I don't think there's a point to this empty,
I don't think there's a beginning or an end.

I've been in a place where not much can reach me.
Even if it's mostly mentally.
An island or oasis,
it's hard to imagine my salvation as anyone else.
Does that make me selfish?

A small beach,
maybe that's where you'll find my body.
Bony fingers stretched out towards something,
probably your general direction.

Wherever that is.

If Anyone Can Hide It, It's Me

Enter the Devoid

Why is everything you say so devoid of emotion?
Like I'm a different person?
You're looking at me like I never meant a single thing to you.

You stepped outside and I have been waiting by the door.
These walls scream when I manage to shuffle by.
They have your voice.

I've been carrying a weight on my back,
it's the things you've said and the drinks I've had.
You know I could never let anything go.

I'm thinking of burning this house down.

If Anyone Can Hide It, It's Me

Aneurysm

You've been an aneurysm lately,
no love,
not much of anything.
Just an ache maybe.

I just wanted to make you feel what I did.
The swelling pressure in my head,
when I heard you gasp.

I shouldn't expect anyone to feel or want the things that I do.

If Anyone Can Hide It, It's Me

Speaking Was Already Hard Enough

You are the twitch in my lip sneaking up on me.
Sudden reminder that I can't talk anymore.
Not about you.
I'll start to speak and pronounce things wrong.
The thought of us made me hesitate.

This mouth is so used to asking for you,
I'm trying to get it together.

I'm trying to shut up.

If Anyone Can Hide It, It's Me

Mourning Breath

What exactly will I taste in the morning?
What will you?
Something acidic or salty?
I hope you can't get it out of your mouth.

Tastes all mix together now,
without you.

I'll wake up and taste you and wish I didn't.

If Anyone Can Hide It, It's Me

All These Plants Want to Be Watered and Live (I Am Not A Plant)

Every organism on this planet has the instinct to survive.
So, I guess I can imagine how it must have felt,
to be with someone who didn't want to be alive.

The only thing I wanted was to hold your hand,
it didn't matter to me if the Sun exploded,
but when I reached for you,
you hurried away.
This says so much more about me than you.

So yes,
you're enjoying the fact that you're right.
That you're right about me.
While I am drinking into unconsciousness,
yet unable to sleep at night.

Whatever you've taken from me,
the absence is what keeps my skin crawling,
it's like that fear when you feel like you're falling.

But all the time.

If Anyone Can Hide It, It's Me

**I'm Not Qualified
To Do Any of These Things for You**

I agree,
I never had much to give you.
Other than my sense of humor and my lips,
but they didn't feel right to yours when we kissed.

And you stopped laughing at my jokes.

Back and Forth

Arousal,
ambition,
the effort it takes to sit still and listen.
They've left me.
It's all gone,
you could count what's still me on one hand.

My eyes are wandering,
small pupils widening.
Nothing looks familiar here.
Most of the time,
I'm wavering,

back and forth.

If Anyone Can Hide It, It's Me

Green

I'm starting to look green around the gills,
good thing it's one of the colors that looks good on me.
Although,
maybe I should be worried about growing gills.

Maybe I should be worried about all this envy,
all this jealousy,
all this green around me.

Connected Distance
(Objects Are Closer Than They Appear)

"Oh man."
Everyone in the world simultaneously sighed.
"What do I do now?"
Again, muttered by everyone.

I'm imagining my pain is shared,
that you all have a mutual understanding,
of its sharpness.

But it's not,
everyone's got their own pain,
or knife in their side,
or back.

Me Imagining You Eating Me Alive

I'll get sick if you look at me directly.
I can feel my stomach in my chest.
You're eating away what's good about me.
My sense of humor is all that's left.

Your bite is paralyzing, venom maybe?
How did my hazel eyes taste?
They haven't been your favorite.
Did my laugh get stuck in your teeth?
I hope I give you heartburn.

I couldn't give you anything else.

If Anyone Can Hide It, It's Me

Thanks

You could swarm,
have the entire hive on attack,
and hurt me in the worst possible way.

And I would probably thank you.

If Anyone Can Hide It, It's Me

Flashy Gifts

Nothing I did was impressive.
I could steal the stars from the sky,
neatly gift wrap and offer them to you.

But you wouldn't flinch,
not even take a second look.

I'm sure the stars are glad I can't touch them.

Dreams That Mean Something

In my dream we both weren't happy,
about each other or where we were.
You were naked but only physically,
I was naked except for my face.

We kissed and it felt rotten.
We kissed and your tongue made mine numb.
We kissed and I didn't feel anything.

On my bed I wrapped my body around yours,
we were both unhappy.

You scream and push me off.
I just looked at you with a blank face,
I didn't understand.

Red string was everywhere,
I don't know what it was supposed to mean,
but we both looked away.

I woke up and was overwhelmed,
I don't want to dream about you anymore.

If Anyone Can Hide It, It's Me

Get Out

Break apart my body from the inside.
Take everything you left here.
Until I am free of you.

Please.

If Anyone Can Hide It, It's Me

Out of Pollen

Your words like bees find their way to me.
I'm allergic.
Hard to hear with all this buzzing.
I'm starting to feel bad,
lethargic.

No sympathy,
please stop stinging me.

If Anyone Can Hide It, It's Me

Burying Your Pets (Burying Yourself)

I'm giving life to something I shouldn't give life too.
My thoughts conjure a sadistic version of you.

I feel like I'm in Pet Sematary,
with everything I'm burying,
hoping they come back to me.

Or maybe I'm a masochist,
to just give suffering your name,
to lead you hand in hand,
and let you follow me around again.

I'll be breathing life into things that should stay dead.
I'll try to bury you head down,
so it's harder for you to climb out.

If Anyone Can Hide It, It's Me

Thinning Me Out
(I'm Pretty Skinny Already)

Make sure to dilute me with water,
until I'm barely here at all.
You'll be able to stand the taste then.
Small sips get bigger again and again.

Everyone says I'm just too much on my own.

Red and Reoccurring

Reaching into my pocket,
Your hair greeted me.

With a forced laugh and an
unenthusiastic smile,
I said **"Hello."**
to everything you ever said,
as I heard it in an instant.

I asked why I would still find you here.
Nine months and four hundred miles away.

Of course,
it didn't have an answer to give me.

Where Is Godzilla When You Need Them?

You're King Ghidorah,
and I am Tokyo.

You'd think,
I would be used to monsters attacking me by now.
But here we are.

Something is always destroying me.

If Anyone Can Hide It, It's Me

Road Runner

The bruises on my knees,
are from begging for things that haven't been there.

The weight of that is an anvil on my head,
except I'm not a cartoon.
But you're still laughing at me like I am.
I've always been one daft duck.

It takes a lot to wake up now,
but what's going to get me out of bed today?
A trip to the bathroom?
Trying to eat?
I can't stomach anything.

The thought of you?
The thought of something that exists,
or doesn't?

Let's spin the imaginary wheel folks.

If Anyone Can Hide It, It's Me

Elbow to Elbow (Just Knee Me in The Head)

I can mouth I'm fine all day,
and people usually believe me.
I can mouth I'm fine all day,
until I picture the small things.
The motions creep up on me,
elbow to elbow and knee to knee.

I'll be feeling great until I think about you,
your elbow to his,
your knee to his.

It's upsetting.

If Anyone Can Hide It, It's Me

You're Gonna Carry That Weight

How many times I wonder,
has someone bared their smile at me with awful intentions?
I want to know every moment someone wanted the worst for me.
I would love to be able to physically hold it,
for it to weigh me down,
and be buried underneath it all.

I want to know how many times you sat awake next to me,
wanting something else.
I want to know how many times you wanted someone else.

He drove you home that night,
so, I guess that's one,

and it's real fucking heavy.

If Anyone Can Hide It, It's Me

Wash You Off Like Dead Skin Cells

I kept washing my face for longer and longer periods of time.
It was autopilot,
I felt like a machine,
circuits exposed but barely still working,
very automatic.

I think I just needed to feel like you never touched me.
The more I scrubbed,
the better I felt about bawling my eyes out in the shower.

Or maybe I was hoping I'd get enough soap in my eyes,
that I'd go blind and panic.
Slipping and slamming my head into the tile.

Either waking up with amnesia,
or never waking up again.

If Anyone Can Hide It, It's Me

I Guess It Doesn't Concern You

Do you feel uncomfortable,
when you see other people's intimacy?
Maybe your skin feels like its being peeled,
or your blood boils?
Do you feel tense or uneasy?

For me it feels external,
something always outside of myself.
Like I've stepped into something I shouldn't be in.
Like I've been removed from the situation.
It's like a plant feels when its uprooted.
A body that's been polluted.

And it's evident,
that both my two cents are spent.
Because I can't afford to think about a damn thing.

What did it feel like to say,
"Maybe that's not what I want."
"It wasn't ever right in the back of my mind."
"I'm not in love with you anymore."

I can tell you how it felt to hear it.

If Anyone Can Hide It, It's Me

This isn't all about her and what happened between us. It's about my growth, it's coming to terms with how I was and how I decided to heal. Do you remember dissecting frogs in high school? Learning what everything did inside the little green body? I've been dissecting us for the last year placing everything I could on the table. I've needed to get a better look. I've always needed to understand. Don't worry I'm taking all the proper safety precautions. I'm wearing gloves, safety goggles and a mask. This is something I can handle.

I took myself out of the frog. I'm learning how I work. I'm studying every detail of myself. Everything I've done wrong is labeled and put in a jar as a reminder. It's easy to look at everyone else and tell them where they're fucking up but when it's me it takes a little more time. There are so many jars to go through.

If the frog was alive, I'm sure it would be happy to have me out of its system. I'm just as happy to have her out of mine. Well, if it was alive, I bet it wouldn't be too happy I'm taking things out of it. It would probably be painful. The need I have to dissect and understand everything makes it all twice as complicated. I'm trying to make sense of and give reason to so much. I can't just be angry, or sad, or happy, or any emotion singularly. It's all happening at once. I'm seeing and feeling everything at once. Must have been overwhelming for the frog. Little frog anxiety attacks. Little frantic frog hopping around its home.

Anyway, I'm singing **"Ribbit, ribbit."** as I'm going through the motions, as I'm looking at all the jars and taking notes. I'm trying to make sense of it all. I'm trying to come out better because of the dissection. It's the least I could do for myself and the frog. **"Ribbit, ribbit."**

If Anyone Can Hide It, It's Me

Act II

I'm seeing red.
I'm fuming.
Fuck you,
him,
and this.

If Anyone Can Hide It, It's Me

I Looked Good on Your Dresser

Your fingertips grazed my whole being,
and my petals twitched.
I blossomed open.

All of existence fits in your hand,
especially me.

Now after you grew tired of my color,
and scent,
you left.

I can't seem to open up again.

How angry I am,
how angry I am at all of this,
especially me.

If Anyone Can Hide It, It's Me

I Saw Your Lips Spell Out His When You Said Mine

Does it sound better when he says your name?
Better than when I did?

Did my voice make you decay?
Did paint chip on the walls,
when I said your name?

I hope it hurts you both when you hear mine.

Optimistic My Ass

My jokes only make me feel worse,
but at least you all get to laugh.
I'll poke fun at the situation,
and feel everyone start to poke back.

I can already see you smile at that,
I'll bleed out all the good and begin losing tact.
I'm told to be optimistic.

I gave you all my energy,
you think I have any left for that?

If Anyone Can Hide It, It's Me

The Second Look

I'll grind my teeth into a smile.

What comes from my killing in kindness?
No one seems to bat an eye.
So, I'll let insolence stem from every one of my pores,
until someone takes a second look.

If I can exert the anger,
if I can apply enough pressure,
do you think I'll feel any better at all?

Warning Signs

In hindsight it makes sense,
no one wants to be touched by someone they don't love.

Although,
you could have told me when you stopped loving me.

Instead of letting me think you did.

You shouldn't stay with someone because you're lonely.

If Anyone Can Hide It, It's Me

Pricked

I know I am wilting,
a stupid flower,
but isn't that okay with you?
My decay?
My head unwilling to accept the loss.
Step on my body again,
these thorns aren't just for show.

I hope I leave a scar.

If Anyone Can Hide It, It's Me

Causality

I sat back and watched all the good,
turn to tragedy.
I'm sure if you asked anyone,
my life looks like a comedy.

But God dammit,
I'm so tired of hearing the laugh track.

This all feels so scripted,
like that funny irony you see on tv.
I'm feeling pretty low.
Are you sure I'm not in some sick sadistic Truman Show?

I'm not as witty as Jim Carrey,
I feel bad for the families watching at home.

If Anyone Can Hide It, It's Me

It Really Isn't

I feel like I lost something,
I'm in the lost and found,
but you found everything.

What did I gain? What did I ask for?
Well after you I can never finish my drinks anymore.

Keep talking to your new feelings,
I hope it works out.
I'll try to let go of mine.
This isn't anything to be upset about.

If Anyone Can Hide It, It's Me

Can Hyrule's Destiny
Really Depend on Such A Lazy Boy?

You called me lazy all the time.
When it felt like someone had stripped all the energy from my
lanky frame because I began to feel low again,
you called me lazy.
When all my ambition for the day balled up into my fingertips
and leaked out of me you scoffed at it.
I wasn't doing nearly as much as you.

My body is attacking itself.
There is a constant war in my intestines,
and it's depleted all available resources.
The iron in me is almost gone.
But me always exhausted and lethargic looked lazy, right?
My brain always dressed in apathy looked lazy, right?
A big part of depression manifests in the inability to do anything,
add that to the persistent draining bite,
of the Crohn's vampire living in me,
and I really gave you something to be proud of, didn't I?

I am always misinterpreted,
because I will never function the same way anyone else does.
You have no idea how it feels to unwillingly pour out the gas
tank and try to do everything on fumes.
I'm trying.

I am fucking lazy,
but don't confuse it with everything else going on.

If Anyone Can Hide It, It's Me

Jokes

I've felt so much like a running joke,
that my feet hurt.

But it's not the only thing that you all laughed about.
You thought it was hilarious when I couldn't let go.
Obvious bruises cover my hands.
I can picture your face,
when our friends kept you up to date.

A piercing cackle escaped your lips,
and every traffic light in the world turned red.

"Fuck you."
Escaped mine.

If Anyone Can Hide It, It's Me

You're Cursed Dude

In the back of your head do you feel me gnawing?
I've whispered a curse to come after you.

I'm mostly at a loss for words,
I didn't expect you to be holding the door.
I didn't expect her to so quickly walk over me,
and into you.

When you look at her,
I hope you feel my teeth,
I hope I still bite.

I hope it never stops aching.

Self-destructive (Scorpio)

You're bored unless you have someone to touch, like me.
You're anxious without something to ruin,
like me.
You're your own worst enemy.
Tripping over your own tail when everything's going well.
October Baby,
make sure you cut it off next time.
If you don't feel up to it,
I can help.

I cut mine off so many times,
It just keeps coming back.

If Anyone Can Hide It, It's Me

Tar and Hostility

Breathe me in like cigarette smoke,
doesn't seem like we're getting any better.
I don't see anything real in your gestures.

I'll sit heavy in your lungs,
like how your heart feels thinking about a certain someone.

And I'm not going away,
you're cursed now.
Feel me melt your brain,
as I get comfy and spread around.
This bruise will get darker.
It's my body now.

If Anyone Can Hide It, It's Me

Silent Seething

It's disgusting how hard you try.
Your mouth running,
any and every compliment drool from it.

Oh God, I hope the fumes are visible.
I'm livid all the time.

Keep your head down when I walk by.

Transparency

I can scrape the love off the walls if you don't like the color.
I know lately we haven't gotten along with one another.
You can see right through me,
but don't think you're the only one.

I'm full of holes,
a ridiculous number of holes.
Anyone could take a look.

Transparency has always been a friend of mine.

It Isn't Personal

My lungs disagree with me and argue,
they want to breathe when I really don't want to.

Something latches on desperate for my affection,
this malice that holds my hand to lead me down the street.
I swear I have a fever or an infection.
Something must be wrong with me.

My mind doesn't mind,
but maybe my eyes do,
they look to the traffic and say I'd look good there too.

I swear I'm just angry at myself.
Can't you tell?
This writing is surgical.
It'll get it all out of me.
This isn't personal.

If Anyone Can Hide It, It's Me

The Day the Earth Stood Still
(But Because Of Me Not Aliens)

The skin on my face is changing colors,
something is spreading throughout me.
The pain accompanied makes me think I'm about to die,
or maybe,
all the anger is just rushing to my head looking for a way out.
I'm about to split for real this time.

The force exerted from my pores,
will be enough to demand the earth stop spinning.
For exactly ten seconds,
everything and everyone will be violently thrown into the
atmosphere.

Everything will stop.
Everything will be out of place,
and I will feel so much better.

If Anyone Can Hide It, It's Me

Throwing Away Your Unwanted Emotions and You

This is something I can force,
and regurgitate.
I'm always looking for an excuse,
to piss you off.

I can throw it all away,
but not when I'm the trash bag.

It's something I can force,
but never want to.

Out of spite,
I'm doing everything you told me not to do.

If Anyone Can Hide It, It's Me

The View Is Better from Him (and Him)

I hope you make new friends,
and you keep falling in love with them.
When your stomach settles but you can't,
you'll jump from one to another again.

Keep trying to find meaning in other people.

If Anyone Can Hide It, It's Me

Are You Even Trying?

I can stomach most things,
even when me and Crohn's are arguing.

But your mediocrity doesn't sit well,
try a little harder.

You're used to making excuses,
I can tell.

Every Dentist Every Tooth

I'd rather,
have all my teeth ripped out,
than have to say any nice thing about you.

I'm every dentists wet dream.

If Anyone Can Hide It, It's Me

I'll Sting You (and Myself) to Death

By the venom in my tail,
be it bitter and unforgiving,
you'll come to realize,
that there is no other intoxication that will bring you closer,
to death,
or ecstasy,

as what crawls and stings,
and latches on to you through me.

No other venom is this violent,
and gentle all at once.

Except mine.

If Anyone Can Hide It, It's Me

Hit Me Until More Than Blood Comes Out

You can't kick the idea from my head now that it's there.
Want to try?
Hit me hard and see what comes out.
I'm eager to see it too.
It's probably not what you'd expect.

The physical manifestation of anger is never what we expect.

If Anyone Can Hide It, It's Me

Enjoy the Taste

They're spraying pesticides on a windy day,
and I hope you're walking by,
mouth open.

No Power but Mine

I refuse to believe the irony that manifests itself,
is the will of some force in the void,
that gets its kicks from poking fun at me.

I'll acknowledge them and admit defeat,
again.

But there is no force or power.
It's just me seeking out anything,
to justify the pain,

and absence.

If Anyone Can Hide It, It's Me

Red as A Newborn (White as A Corpse)

Honestly,
If we're being honest,
I don't think you were ever honest enough.

Always glorifying the past,
no wonder I didn't measure up,
and why nothing sparked from a kiss or a touch.
It's okay,
we always want what we can't have,
want what we used to have.
Nostalgia is your Achilles' heel.

Everybody lies,
or has something they feel they have to hide.

I'll try not to hold it against you.

If Anyone Can Hide It, It's Me

Bleach

I can't wait,
until it starts to deteriorate.
You're going to realize how brittle you are.
How you've molded your lovers into a first-aid kit.
Bandaging your skin, proud.
You just keep trying to fix yourself.

Acid rain will start to fall on your idea of love,
and I bet it stings.

I will remain,
a reminder in the worst parts of your brain.
Or on your favorite white t-shirt,
a coffee stain.

You won't be able to bleach me out.

If Anyone Can Hide It, It's Me

Kerosene! Gasoline!
(Get the Lice I Named After You Off Me)

Covering myself in kerosene,
and you're chugging down some gasoline.

I just wanted to smell like anything other than you.
While you've kept saying you're freezing on the inside
swallowing a match too.

You finally found something that could keep you warm.
Try not to complain when it starts to burn.

I know I won't.

If Anyone Can Hide It, It's Me

The Last Time

Leaking inconsistency,
I can't take you seriously.
Why are you asking *me* anything specifically?

Decide what you want to do with yourself,
before you start touching me.

If Anyone Can Hide It, It's Me

No water

I want to get to a point,
where I feel like I don't need to be kept warm.
Where hands don't terrify me,
and the pain in my stomach doesn't make me dizzy.

I want my cold to feel comfortable.
I want your warmth to feel foreign.
I want to feel the emotional distance impact my body,
hitting me like a train that's been late all morning.

Where I am now is craving,
it's anger,
it's a fever that's not breaking,
it's dehydration,
and there's no water here.

So, fuck me,
right?

If Anyone Can Hide It, It's Me

Prosopagnosia

I can't wait until Prosopagnosia is available in pill form.
I'll stop recognizing everyone from high school.
I'll stop feeling the need to hide in public.
You'll come up to me,
and I won't know who the fuck you are.

And I hope I've been drinking.
And I hope I slur and spit when I talk.
So what I say isn't the only disrespectful thing you remember.

When you remind me who you are I'm going to laugh.

If Anyone Can Hide It, It's Me

It Matters Less the More You Think About It (And How Everything Is Just Matter Anyway)

You believed in soulmates,
you still do.
Sorry if I have to break it to you,
but that isn't how this works.

You want to believe your life is scripted,
anything to justify,
anything to get away with it.

I'm going to have to oppose that,
nothing was made specifically for you or me.

Or anyone for that matter.
We're all just the product of chemicals,
that existed at the right time and place to hurt each other.
The microwave had just the right settings for you to be born.

Stop taking yourself so seriously.

If Anyone Can Hide It, It's Me

One of the most defining moments of my healing process was when I fled to Tallahassee. I needed to get away from where it all happened. So, I scheduled off work and guilt tripped a close friend into coming with me. Then I was off to stay with friends in Tally, the promised land that kept her eyes away from me. A change of scenery is what I thought I needed but really the changes had to occur inside of me. For anything to heal I needed to change in so many ways.

Now, the following things I discuss in this section of the book I do not encourage anyone to partake in. This is just what I decided to do. Most people won't agree with my choices but that's okay because they're mine.

Where I was mentally, I simply wanted to erase who I was. Hand all of my friends the big eraser for big mistakes and let them have at it! I wanted to start over. I couldn't handle being the person that she left. I couldn't handle being the person I had always been. So, what I decided to do was buy a huge amount of psychedelic mushrooms from a friend and eat them to change completely. This just seemed like the best thing to do!

A lot of my friends have had experience with psychedelics and I always heard about them going through complete personality overhauls. I did my research and read up plenty about them helping people with PTSD and their depression. My overdramatic self not able to deal with the pain, I decided it was the better option rather than feeling my emotions. It was a better option than just drowning myself in alcohol too! Nothing else was going on in my life, so I figured, why not?

So, upon arriving to Tallahassee me and a friend ate a moderate dosage and we sat and talked. Thinking about it now I feel bad that I completely directed his 'trip' due to my emotional instability, but what can you do? The whole time I was anxious

If Anyone Can Hide It, It's Me

and feeling awful, but as it started to take effect, I began to feel lighter. I began laughing and I felt amazing. I started seeing the walls breathe and colors appearing where they shouldn't. Me and one of my closest friends started comparing everything we saw when something in the back of my head shifted and I began to think about my relationships and my life and my ex. Everything was tumbling down, baby.

Something they don't really tell you about the mushrooms, or what my friends didn't tell me, is how much they make you think. I started to think myself a bit insane, which now I understand your *'trip'* is going to be determined by your emotional state, and boy was I in a *bad* place. I ran up the stairs to be alone in a room to think about what I was doing wrong with my life. It wouldn't stop, it was on repeat. It was like I was able to step outside of myself and view my actions unbiased. I wasn't letting myself get away with anything. All the things I had ever done and not done were manifesting as humanoid shapes that formed a judge and jury to watch me shake in a fetal position.

When my friends found me and asked me how I was I finally admitted something that I never had before. They asked me if I really wanted to spend my time doing this. If I wanted to have fun or wallow in my sadness. I remember looking at them crying my eyes out and saying that I wanted to die. Not just in that moment but in general. I finally said it and it wasn't a self-deprecating joke! I was honest. I was honest about never understanding how people wanted to be alive. I was honest about never feeling that lust for life. It was like something had finally opened in my chest, my ribcage ripping apart and everything started spewing out of it. After some hugs and them talking me down they played me some music and sat with me as I cried and screamed out at everything, talking wildly about my ex.

If Anyone Can Hide It, It's Me

    I had talked about it beforehand, but it was like my words actually meant something this time. I can't recall another time I felt so emotionally there. Like a veil wasn't in between me and my words and my emotions. I felt everything! I was able to get it all out and walk out of that room feeling better than I had ever felt. I was completely enamored at the little mushrooms that got those feelings out of me. We spent the rest of the day running around the city and laughing and having a great time. It was exactly what I needed.

    I won't go over every single time I've eaten them; I'll just say that you'll notice the changes in my poetry and how it affected me. Every time I ate them, I noticed small changes in myself. I was becoming more aware of my patterns and problems and what I needed to do to fix them. I became more aware that it was me all along, that my problems had stemmed from not nourishing myself and staying stagnant and being held back by past trauma. It became less about her and more about me. More about building from the pain instead of succumbing to it. It helped me realize deep down I did want things for my life.

    After spending those few weeks in Tallahassee, and again this is not me recommending any of you take the route I did, I started to regularly use psychedelics. For months I would set aside a day to myself and use either mushrooms or LSD. I considered it a form of therapy where I would either seclude myself alone in my room and spend hours thinking about my life or with my friends discussing the universe and our place in it. I felt as if I had done it and I had changed. I had become so much more empathetic and understanding to myself and others.

    This didn't come without repercussions however, there were negative effects that I had dealt with for a while. I feel that if you tamper with your perception of reality for long enough, it

If Anyone Can Hide It, It's Me

becomes harder to figure out what is real and not. For a long time, I was disassociated. You could ask a lot of people that saw me going through different phases, I was acting quite strange! It was like I was being turned upside down and seeing all the awful things that I'd done or said leak out of me. I watched every bad decision I made on a loop with an awful soundtrack. I was forced to call myself out on my bullshit and make a list of things I had to repair about myself. I went through some bad times while abusing these substances, but I was able to develop even more and heal because of it. I've read that the brain has a difficult time determining the difference between hallucinations, vivid intense emotions, and actual experiences. That a lot of the time it registers them the same way. I was able to go through these amazing emotional and awful ominous places and come back to a more complete me.

    The first time I took LSD I felt so full of love that I exclaimed loudly it was the answer to everything. I was crying at the overwhelming emotions I felt and yelled that love and compassion and empathy was the answer to everything. My sober and not so sober friends laughed at me, but I felt amazing. I felt as if doors to my emotions that had been locked swung open and hit me in the face. I found all the emotional wounds not dealt with in the past and I'm working on them now.

    I understand the stigma on psychedelics. I want you to know that, for me at least, they helped. It's okay if you want to dismiss it as nothing more than a stupid kid using drugs as a coping mechanism, because essentially that's what it was. I was stupid and reaching for anything to feel better, but I'm being honest when I say I feel so much better. Sorry mom! Sorry dad! I love you!

If Anyone Can Hide It, It's Me

Act III

She really messed you up,
or were you always this way?
Either way,
go ahead,
nothing else matters.
Set yourself on fire,
and make sure everyone sees.
Go fucking crazy.

If Anyone Can Hide It, It's Me

Cliché

You kissed me from a distance,
making sure I couldn't see how far you were.
You pushed my hand away when it reached for yours.

It drove me mad.

So now I keep everyone a certain length away.
I cannot support them,
I am too afraid.

Your hands kept me at a distance,
now mine shake too much to carry anyone.
I don't want to hold you all on my fingertips,
at the ready to let go.

I will pull back.

If Anyone Can Hide It, It's Me

Like the Seasons Th(i)ngs Changed

Your voice used to put me to sleep,
and try not to think of that as an insult.
Seldom does anything ever help me rest.

No longer is it a whisper caressing,
or kissing my ears.
It's now a shrill scream,
echoing in the back of my mind.

Keeping me awake at night.

If Anyone Can Hide It, It's Me

Myodesopsia

I still see you haunt the places I crawl into.
Where I go to rest or to laugh.
My peripheral will catch you there.

You're usually never looking at me.

Let Me Know

I measure myself,
in people I've touched,
and moments I've lost.
Opportunities that fell through my hands.
I'm not sure how to stop this,
where my mouth and my mind run.
Why can't I get my feet to?

If you have any ideas,
let me know.

I (Don't) Want to Touch

The thought of calling anyone beautiful,
puts a deeper pit in my already inflamed stomach.
And thinking of anything resembling intimacy,
is sickening.

It's a fickle feeling.
Wanting to touch and then not.
Wanting to be touched and then not.

I don't have the time of day to worry about this,
but I still do.

What else could be on my mind really?

Animal Parts

I'm made up of so many things that ask for more,
and no one has the right parts I'm asking for.

The animal in me is always hungry.
I'll lose my head and crawl on all fours,
screaming at whatever walks by.

But that's what this makes us do isn't it?

I've just had too much time to develop this,
all the things snuck into my mind.
Taking over my body one at a time.

Who put me here?
The world just happens right?
Was it me?

I didn't think you were enough to make me like this,
but here I am.

Viscum Album

My existence is parasitic,
I am the weeds that wrap around plants.
Smothering others,
making sure nothing is left,
it's necessary simply to see myself.

Clinging to them,
clenching in my hands,
not out of respect or love.
But to declare, **"I am here, I am happy."**
But to destroy.

Without a flower for my vines to suffocate and devour,
I cannot feel myself.

With you gone,
I will starve and die.

The Greyhound Bus

Maybe this bridge will collapse,
I won't have to worry anymore.
I'm sure I'd be unlucky enough to stay intact.

I'm watching all the cars imagining crashes,
I didn't think I was this bad.
I've tried to sleep on this bus for hours, but I can't,
I'm not even thinking about anything in particular.

My eyes just won't stay closed,
I keep looking for something,
nothing in particular.

The Aftertaste Won't Last Forever (Hopefully)

Do you want to watch me indulge?
I'm out of my mind lately,
and all the things I do aren't helping.
Tell me how I lash out violently at nothing.

You seem distracted,
you seem distant.
Don't you want to see me split in two in an instant?

Please let these toxic things I got my hands on,
end the conversations I have with my reflection

Every night.
Every night.
Every night.

If Anyone Can Hide It, It's Me

Pathetic

Sitting alone I cried at the silence,
it was enough to break me down.
Every noise that escaped the walls,
or outside,
entered me and I felt anxious.

I couldn't shake out what made its way into me.
As it tore into my nerves I swayed about,
I couldn't sit still I kept pulling at my hair,
biting my hands to calm down.

This happened for no reason.
I just couldn't stop.
I'm so afraid this is me now,
I'm so afraid this was me all along.

And you just kept it at bay,
now you are a part of what creeps inside me.

Sick

Some of my clothes don't fit right,
I feel like I've lost weight,
like I haven't eaten in days.

My skin is too crowded, a room full.
Uncomfortable,
I'm sharing it,
with every dark thing imaginable.
I feel them brush against the surface baring their teeth.

I'll catch myself mumbling from time to time.
I can't tell if it's me or them.
Can you?

I can't gather the strength to leave here,
my body is heavy and doesn't want to move.

I feel sick.

If Anyone Can Hide It, It's Me

Which Is Making Me Bleed Crohn's or The Thought of You?

I'm tired of seeing all this blood come out of me.
Its stress kindling the sparks of my inflammation.
This is something you said or something I ate.
I'll wake up and reluctantly,
you're usually the first thing on my mind.
If I'm finally going to die of blood loss is the second.

It might be wishful thinking,
to think that we were anything other than what we were.
We aren't written in the stars.
We are just narcissistic bags of bones and meat and lard.
And it's hard yet so easy to miss you.

It's really putting a flame in my belly,
making my insides feel like molten lava jelly.

It's nothing to worry about,
I'm pretty tame.
And I've got plenty of drugs to numb the pain,
to fill up the space of what's leaving me.
I'm hoping it's you and all the things you left in me.
But I'm not that lucky unfortunately.

It All Feels the Same

My equilibrium seems to be rotting away,
and I've set foot into delirium.
Instead of balance I'm filled with vertigo.
No sense of direction,
I've got nowhere to go.

It all feels the same,
everyone's lack of personal space,
and the insecurities that find their way to my face.

Point me to sensibility,
I have to take responsibility.
Is this an anxiety attack,
or a caffeine headache?
Hello, do you have an answer?

Good or bad everything feels the same!

If Anyone Can Hide It, It's Me

Did I Become So Fragile? (Or Have I Always Been?)

I rarely think about it,
I fill my day with distraction.
But occasionally,
a memory flashes in my head.

Something we did,
or you said.
I grit my teeth,
as every ounce of me wanders off and gets lost.

It only takes a second,
it only lasts a couple more.

It's so easy for you to destroy me.

If Anyone Can Hide It, It's Me

Clumsy (I Don't Want Any More of This)

Are you aware,
or awake?
I've been walking for days,
next to venomous snakes.

I misstep and crush their heads all the time.

I apologize,
am I made up of an apology?
Is that all I'm worth,
a bad analogy?

The heat is leaving my yellow body.
I felt more like a hobby,
than your lover.

So Funny

It's funny what little things come back to haunt you.
I'm not afraid to get soap in my eyes.
Parts of me burn all the time.
I'm afraid of seeing your ghost in the shower,
asking me to move over,
asking me to share the hot water.

The little spirits that fly around me,
that carry spiteful memory.
I must look so funny,
swatting at nothing.

So funny.

If Anyone Can Hide It, It's Me

What I Ate and Will Again

Floating on the floor,
I could feel myself melt into the carpet.
I put a lot in my body that didn't belong in it.

Feeling like someone put my head underwater,
or that my body was a tree,
termites chewing.
My whole existence is stretched thin.

Your name, mine, and his.
I spent the last few hours screaming.
Incoherently unhinged,
finally feeling something.

I'm not there yet but these things in me:
the termites, the inner workings,
my unfortunate unrequited feelings.
Eventually won't have their teeth in me.

What I ate and will again will probably eat me.
Chewing and swallowing my senses,
I'm sure they'll get me there.

Wherever *there* is.

I Couldn't Tell You What I'm Looking For

I'm not looking for anything physical,
my sense of touch is reluctant now.

I guess I'm looking for stability,
but in everything I dip myself into,
I end up finding nonexistent sides of myself.

I can't explain how nerve-wracking my constant search feels,
only to lead to nothing.

This endless ticking in my clock head is inconvenient,
quite the hindrance it's been.
I'm just waiting for the gears to stop,
maybe that's what it means to be content.

Maybe I'm just looking for an end.

If Anyone Can Hide It, It's Me

Emotional Demands
(And Where You Can Dispose of Them)

I've been thinking a lot about this last year.
How nothing has left an impression.
That most things are never clear.
How I feel so much more comfortable with the taste of beer,
over the taste of anyone else.

Like my days are topsy-turvy,
while everyone's scrambling,
lost their heads and common courtesy.
I'll sit not so pretty,
mumbling everything you could describe as 'petty'.
Never seemed like the universe had anything to give to me,
especially mercy.
But it's not like I'm asking,
More often than not I'm just relaxing.
I can't remember the last time it didn't feel like I was simply passing,
up on every opportunity that slapped me in the face.

Like I'm circling the drain down to my mistakes.
Like I've got all the time imaginable to waste.
Like I'm letting all the love I could feel slip away.
Like everything I do is underneath a certain feeling I can't escape.

But everyone tells me I'm alright.
Everyone tells me that It's alright.
Why can't I shake the feeling that it's not?

I'm Evaporating

I've been having a lot of panic attacks.
I feel like fluid ever changing.
We can't decide what shape to take.

Am I solid today?
Will I evaporate?

There's not enough water,
It feels like it's all leaving me.

I don't have anything left,
I'm drying up.

If Anyone Can Hide It, It's Me

Corroding and Controlling

While you've been gone,
something cold has sank into my chest.
A sigh left my lips when it began to spread.
You could see my breath,
or maybe only I can?

I feel its hands grip.
I feel it make its way to my head.

Just like you,
it swims through so easily.

When it reaches my head,
will you finally be done with me?
Could I sleep without this constant tug?

Or will it simply grasp my brain and squeeze until I die?

Life in Routine (Stop the Ride Please)

I'm sour,
not expecting good things.
You wanted something sweet to eat.

I'm elastic,
stretch me please,
snapping me back to better again.

God damn.

Where have I been?
I don't know who I am.
Everything seems rehearsed.
It's not your fault I'm making this worse.

I keep asking why I do anything?
Why do I wake up a new person every day?
It's harder to think with all these heads,
to remember why I say anything.

When will I get to dissipate?

If Anyone Can Hide It, It's Me

Residual

These lights won't go away.
Did I walk too far?
Sink too deep?
I feel as if I understand now,
why certain wolves dress as sheep.

I can feel my fangs turn to teeth.
Still looking for you,
I hate how you won't look at me.

I'll use your toothbrush and your jacket.
Lick my wounds until I can't stand it.
I'll waste my time and I'll walk alone outside.

And I'll find wolves that are dressed as wolves,
I'll eat them as they eat me.
You won't be able to tell us apart.

There won't be anything left.
I welcome it.

Reality Is

It's getting worse.
It's getting harder to determine,
what's real between what I've seen,
what I've done, what I've heard or said,
and what I play over and over in my head.

The light won't fade,
I keep unplugging the lamp.

I've lost touch with most things I used to touch.
They don't seem to miss me,
my fingers don't seem to miss them.

I keep telling myself it's all temporary,
that I'll wake up eventually.
We all have something that keeps us together,
reality or dreaming?

If Anyone Can Hide It, It's Me

Am I awake (Or is this a Dream?)

What's the key to feeling alive?
Lately I've been wondering.
I find myself in between being asleep and awake.
Nothing has made me feel filled with life.

My vision is fading slowly.
Days go by and I feel as if I'm waiting,
to swing open the door to consciousness,
or close and lock it into sleep.

But no one feels like coffee,
no one feels like rest.
Everything feels like disruption,
and I'm trying my best.

But it's not working out.

If Anyone Can Hide It, It's Me

Vultures

Feed your ego,
your appetite is appealing or even appalling.
I can hear vultures circling,
their beaks calling and squawking.

If you reap what you sow,
then what have I sown?
I haven't planted anything worth mentioning.
Nothing really fits together,
none of my seeds want to grow.

Is their circling above me my own doing?
Do the vultures know what they'll reap?
Has what I've sown earned me a place in their beak?

My body doesn't have much to offer,
but they can have it.
Finish off my head first,
make sure you crack the skull,
make sure you chew my ego dead.

If Anyone Can Hide It, It's Me

Your Curiosity Isn't Sincere

My derangement tiptoes around everyone else.
No one notices.
If anyone can hide it,
it's me.

I've been stepping on eggshells for years,
hiding wherever I can.
All the balancing acts have made me dizzy.
This pressure on my spine from your glares,
is really starting to affect me.

This constant itch in my fingertips,
when I see you or your condescending smile,
it all feels all too familiar.

When everything else in my life doesn't.

If Anyone Can Hide It, It's Me

Keep Your Distance

Nothing good comes out of me now,
every bit of malice is oozing out.

I'm not looking for an answer in this place.
I'm not looking for you.

Whatever hands come for me,
are more attractive and more charming than you could ever be.

And when the force twists my body bruised,
I'm sure it will never go away.
Holding onto me is something worse.

Keep your distance.

If Anyone Can Hide It, It's Me

Daily Doubt, Weekly Woe, and Yearly Yearn

About one hundred layers of uncertainty,
taking my time more importantly.
Figuring out the difference between me now and me yesterday.

It's at question why and what comes out of my subconscious.
Explain what I mean when I say:
"I don't want this."
I'm bubbling underneath the surface.
Ready to pop.
But what's to want in the current of small talk?
I'd rather be carried away in the madness of what I am and what I am not.
Keep yapping away about the weather, I get it:
It's hot.

I don't know why I'm expected to pay attention to what's coming out of your mouth.
I've got worse things inside of me to figure out.
But the damage in my head and to environment,
I'm trying my best not to say, **"Fuck it."**
while growing tired of this.
The feeling is delusion and I'm falling further into the illusion.
When am I going to feel real?

When does the curtain fall on the constant ache?
When does the acting end?

If Anyone Can Hide It, It's Me

Over Drinking! Over Thinking! (Over This Bullshit)

Am I doing a bad job?
Have I been doing enough?
Everybody says that I think too much.

There isn't really a way to turn it off,
and I ask myself how you're not all consumed by your thoughts.

I'll pour out every fiber of what makes me up,
and have to apologize for it.
How are you all so well put together?

Or maybe all my *'together'* isn't here anymore.

If Anyone Can Hide It, It's Me

I Really Need to Go to The Store

I am officially out of shampoo.
Well, I've been out for two weeks now.
I've just been squeezing the bottle,
trying to force out enough to get by.
It's the same way I squeeze my body,
hoping it's enough to get by.

The bottle is as empty as me on the days where I feel empty.
This happens more than I'd like to admit.

I can walk into the grocery store,
I can always get more shampoo.
I just haven't had the energy to even think about it.

I'll get more,
but how long am I going to have to squeeze me,
hoping something comes out?

What am I going to do when nothing does?

If Anyone Can Hide It, It's Me

Who's in My head Now?

Crying out for anything warm,
I scurry back into myself.
Little devil in my tongue,
keeps spitting my words out.

"His or mine?"

I'm not going to do anything,
I'm standing neutral,
when a decision has to be made.
And all I've done is let time slip away.
My hands are always idle.

Losing track of where I left my body,
something else finds their way to it.
I don't believe in Satan,
but this feeling has to be similar,
I'm feeling pretty awful,
an awfully attractive bitter.

I don't think anything is being decided by me,
however,
nobody likes a quitter.

Daydream Eulogy

How often do you think about your own death?
I feel like it's a common thing,
at least imagining your funeral.

I see you there,
in the pews or outside.
You're always crying,
and I guess I'm happy that you're always crying.

Everyone thinks about death,
so, I feel less crazy when I do.
When the sugar dipped words,
come out of your cavity filled mouths,
I think my hands might twitch in the grave.

For the most part,
you all have such nice things to say.

If Anyone Can Hide It, It's Me

I'm Going Crazy

I can't tell if it's you or the constant pain in my teeth,
that's driving me insane.
But is there a difference in this interference?
Feels like my head's splitting.
I wonder what's going to come out.
Something with eyes?

Or will I end up in a room screaming,
waiting for something else to scream back?

But it's just going to be you.

If Anyone Can Hide It, It's Me

The Taste Will Remind Me of You

I've been thinking of filling my cavities with glue,
because nothing I say seems to stick.
Because I've got nothing better to do.
All the trouble I apparently cause,
none of my adhesive covered words can fix it.

I'm hoping I can hot glue the sad and pathetic,
back into the holes in my teeth.
It's so embarrassing for me,
what I give you to look at and what you have to see.

It'll numb the pain,
but I don't think it'll last long.

Continental Shift

In and out of a haze I can't find myself very well.
Seems like no matter how much time passes,
it feels like a blur.
That week felt like a day,
a month felt like a week.

I don't know how to place myself in any situation anymore.
I walked onto a stage,
the color scheme is for a sitcom,
but I'm dressed for a murder mystery,
or a Lifetime original tragedy.

I keep feeling like a dim light,
my fuse is about to go out.
There's a continental shift in my bones.

My planet is going to look so different when this is done.

If Anyone Can Hide It, It's Me

Pushover

Pushover.
You could push me over so easily.
It's the way I'm always standing.
It's because I weigh nothing.
I'm not comparable to anything.

I'm such a pushover,
you can push over this head of mine.

With the way I've let everything happen,
with the way I've felt like nothing.

Completely Constructed

I think I'll be chasing that feeling forever.
Tripping over my feet every time I ingest.
I hate how everything you like is still in my head,
I hate how I can't feel complete without keeping my habits fed.

I realize my chest has been opened,
and hands have come out,
clawing toward everything around me.
This vacancy is relentless.
It has been building,
what you see in me is what it's constructed.

I am a perfect persona,
made of traits I absorbed from everyone else.
One tear in the threads and I come apart.

I can't hide anymore.

Pruning

I sat fixated,
until the water grew cold,
on my pruning fingers.

Intertwined like vines,
I couldn't help but think they resembled thorns.
Thorns that would trap anything they came across.

Now,
like ice clinging to my body.
I couldn't avoid the notion,
that despite the approach,
be it to maim or caress,
everything they touch,
in some way,
will bleed.

If Anyone Can Hide It, It's Me

Everyday Anxious!

I will continue to feel anxious,
as the black spots in the corner of my eyes move around.
You couldn't tell though.
My eyesight has never been better.
These glasses are five years old and it's never been better.

I will dart back and forth like everything else in the room.
I have to keep up the pace with everyone here.
I'm playing the game you play when you're still breathing.
Constant pros and cons are weighed in my head on the subject.
I am a plastic ball full of hamsters,
I'm starting to feel crowded and uncomfortable,
but you all look so relaxed.

Often, I wonder if my heads playing tricks on me when someone starts up a conversation.
Are you real or have the black spots morphed into human form?
Would anyone actually say that?
Either way, you're awful at small talk.
I am continuously getting worse at small talk.
I am continuously getting worse.
But my eyesight has never been better.
Even if the spots cover the plastic ball.
Even if I am allergic to hamsters.
Even if keeping pace makes me want to die and slowing down does the same.
Even if all I have is small talk.
My eyesight has never been better.

If Anyone Can Hide It, It's Me

You're Gone! I'm Gone!

Parts of me miss you,
or maybe just the moments you're tied to.

I'm realizing how little I care about anything,
and how almost everyone feels draining.

Like my mouth is sore from talking about the weather,
and no matter how under an influence I am,
I never feel better.

Because even if I miss you,
all of what we were was self-inflicting,
and now I know I don't want any of it.

I just want the inside of me to make sense again.

If Anyone Can Hide It, It's Me

Whole//Hole

I heard you loved another boy while you were with me.
That you had him in mind kissing me.
I'm water and I'm boiling,
anger turning to steam.
I'm disappearing.

It explains how every time you touched me it was only half,
but I mistakenly saw the whole.
It explains how every time I touched you it felt like my hand was
going through a hole.

I'm still reaching out in what feels endless.
You know I can't tell if I like it,
or if I've had enough of this.

Should I be afraid?
This is finally starting to feel comfortable!

Growing (But Violent)

I'm garden grown,
but the soil is rotten.

You might get nauseous getting too close.
I can't imagine how you'd feel if you touched me.
A little worse than agony most likely.

I'm still growing,
but I don't think this rot is going to come out.

I Don't Know What Color I Am

Looks like you're lost,
acting like a chameleon,
eyes in each direction.
Colors interchangeable,
never really aspired for perfection.

It's okay to hide sometimes,
when nothing around you feels alright.
Just don't forget what color you really are.

If Anyone Can Hide It, It's Me

Like the Infected Tooth You'll Be Taken Out Too

I don't think about you anymore,
unless I'm on some sort of substance.
When something creeps up behind me,
grabs my shoulders,
and whispers your name.

But usually day to day you no longer exist.
You do not plague me anymore.
I plague myself.

It was here before you and it will be here after.
Just as I carry no place in you.
You are fading from me.

If Anyone Can Hide It, It's Me

    I'm finally starting to understand where she was emotionally when we first started dating. Not that it really matters now, but I believe comprehension of any situation is incredibly important. I'm filled with the desire to know the why's and the how's. What makes me assume I know how she felt is that I'm probably in the exact same place now. I clearly remember her complaints on being connection starved. We grew closer at a very optimal time. It didn't hurt that a decent amount of history and chemistry existed between us. Sparking a tiny flame on our friendship. I was there. That's all it was, and it made me more appealing as a romantic interest. People are there for us at convenient times. It happens when we are more susceptible to it. More susceptible to falling for whatever is there. Falling for whatever distracts us from ourselves.

    I'm learning how easy it is to fall into a catacomb of perplexing emotions when your hearts demands aren't exactly being met. I've been walking around aimlessly in them for a while now, and I'm trying not to use other people as candles to find my way around. Although, I think I was more like a match for her with how quick the flame went out. Maybe even a canary to make sure she wouldn't end up walking down the wrong path and start coughing. A canary to warn her of all the tunnels full of poisonous gas, or could it be that I was the poisonous gas?

    Right now, I think about all the times where it was necessary for me to change for her to be happy. I'll admit a lot of me wasn't ideal. A large part of me sucked! We all suck. I was depressed and being dragged down by past trauma I didn't want to deal with. I never admitted it, but it made me come to a standstill. She didn't see me going anywhere and neither did I.

If Anyone Can Hide It, It's Me

What a fool I've made of myself! A fool to think that any of it was as important as I made it out to be. I was wrong. I was dramatic. I was stupid to let myself attach to her the way I did. I was stupid to think I'd die when she left. However, no one knows any better. If I had built more of myself, I would have had more to fall back on.

In hindsight, and wearing not so rose-colored glasses, I can see where she was. I can understand that she was just frantically looking around the house for a band-aid. Shuffling around to find something to cover up and distract herself.

At least that's what I've gathered from my perspective. We never really know what's going on with someone else. We can only project ourselves onto them. We only understand what we understand. I just have the evidence at hand and my own intuition, but who knows, my intuition, perspective and paranoia may be my very own band-aid.

If Anyone Can Hide It, It's Me

It's been a little while since the apocalypse. Well not exactly, I think everyone would have noticed if the Earth cracked in two. There was no end of the world, it was just me separating violently. It was just me. It was my inability to handle the ending of a relationship. It was me throwing my weight and frustration around.

I may have had a hard time because of everything, but I'm feeling better now. I'm trying to be kind even when I am hurt. I'm growing furiously like a weed from all the destruction. Thank you.

If Anyone Can Hide It, It's Me

Act IV

Well,
you spent a lot of time whining,
and confused.
And hurt.
And doing stupid shit.
You figured out that it's more about you.
Every lesson really has to be beat hard into you,
doesn't it?

If Anyone Can Hide It, It's Me

  I want to elaborate on a certain theme that may be recurring in some of my poems. That theme being when I say I am two, or that I have two faces or heads. Besides just being born with cleft lip and palate and looking like slightly different people depending on the angle your eyes catch me, for months I couldn't really figure out if what I was doing was me or not. I had no idea what made me happy or who I was. Nothing felt right, like everything I knew I enjoyed was erased. Thinking about it now, it was me just becoming newly single after a relationship that lasted about three years in my early twenties. Growing with someone, and then that someone is gone, leaves you feeling lost. You could assume I was being dramatic again. Although, I just figured it was due to all the psychedelic use that unearthed more of me than I ever knew. That it was just me learning about myself.

  My brain felt like it was readjusting, and I was on autopilot. I would be out drinking with friends and co-workers and it would hit me in the middle of a great time, and I would disassociate. I would fall into a sort of trance and begin asking myself what I truly wanted. Was this it? Sometimes it felt as if I wasn't really in control. Like I was on the sidelines and this other me was out doing things. I'm yelling from the back of the car, but another me doesn't turn around. The other me does not heed my warnings about oncoming traffic.

  I've kind of always felt fragmented by how I acted with people and how I thought. I would go on the whole day as different personas that I didn't even recognize. I mean everyone feels this way, right? I guess for me I had some wires crossed. However, for the last five or six months it was relentlessly gnawing at me, all the mouths were hungry and taking bites. It had gotten worse and it felt like I was deteriorating. I couldn't

If Anyone Can Hide It, It's Me

figure out what was really me. I was just split into two different people, each fighting over the wheel. Nothing I did seemed like it was up to me. I wasn't the protagonist anymore. I kept telling myself I was thinking about it too hard, that no one should really spend this much time questioning if what they were doing was making them happy. Everyone else kept telling me the same thing. *'You're thinking too much.'* Maybe they aren't thinking enough!

Eventually I came to the realization that everything I did was a part of this *'me'* I was looking for. That this was my head letting go of the past three years, it was me adjusting to the change. The two different heads that kept barking orders at each other were still on the same body. I am every different part of me that conflicts with the other. After that, it wasn't so hard to just let myself be in the moment or to stop questioning everything I was doing. It wasn't so much that I was thinking too hard about it, I just needed to come to terms that it isn't always easy being a person. We aren't simple at all and occasionally different parts of us fight. My right arm never agrees with my left!

I still get caught up in the idea sometimes that my heads aren't screwed on tight enough but that's what makes me myself, right? I'm falling apart a lot of the time, but I can always bring myself back together. Even if I have multiple heads, they all belong to me.

If Anyone Can Hide It, It's Me

Repercussions

It's become apparent,
how important these moments are,
when I stumble into a place where you still live.
If I'm drunk on the bathroom floor,
or when my mind is falling apart in my hands.
As my whole sense of self begins to divide,
I've stepped into where you've been lingering.

It's important to let this feeling overtake me,
to untangle you from myself.

It's always been so hard for me to be vulnerable.

If Anyone Can Hide It, It's Me

I'm Laughing Too

I feel unlovable.
I won't say it's because of you.
But I think everyone knows.

It's scary because it's not painful,
it's just a mouthful,
and I'm tired of talking about it.

Head in hand,
I could hear you making a joke.
It's what I am,
a punchline and a laugh.

So happy to hear you've been laughing for the past year.

If Anyone Can Hide It, It's Me

Irony and You (Lemons Not Included)

I'm covered in wounds,
and irony's lemon juice.
At least I've always liked the taste.

Sour things appeal to me,
and unsurprisingly,
so does the sting.

If Anyone Can Hide It, It's Me

The Ship's Name is Distraction

I live for the distraction,
but is that really being alive?
Do you know how that feels?
Do you know what that's like?

I think about one day things falling into place,
I think about if that exists for anyone,
or if this confused look is permanent on my face.

I ask people what makes them happy,
to find out the secret,
to cut the bullshit conversation,
to see if it can help me.

I want to know if this feeling ever goes away,
or if it just depends on what and who,
I interact with that day.

I'm wondering if anyone is telling the truth,
or if we're all pretending.
I'm trying to figure out if this is just me,
or depression,
or the lack of connection?
Surrounded by everyone,
I feel like I'm on an island.

Waiting for a ship to sail by.

If Anyone Can Hide It, It's Me

Death Ain't a Joke Baby (But Life Is Certainly One)

Even if they're backwards I'm still taking steps,
whoever said forward was a good thing?

Maybe I want to deteriorate a little,
before leaping toward anything important,
before forcing myself to feel again.

A dying tree still gives you air to breathe,
roadkill still gives birds something to eat.
Death makes up for wasted space someway.

While I'm falling apart what will I contribute?
Anything at all?
I hope so.

Death and life are the same,
either or,

I'm still me!

If Anyone Can Hide It, It's Me

Talking to Me (Drinking You)

Amid all the other voices,
the laughs,
and sighs,
Tequila whispered to me,
"Why bother?"

I gulped you down and agreed,
why bother?

If Anyone Can Hide It, It's Me

Not Listening to Your Intuition

I don't get stabbed in the back.
I get stabbed,
on every bit of visible surface something sharp could fit.
Mostly my face.

I usually always see it coming but never take any precaution.
I'll see motivation spark as a hand reaches for a knife.
"They're really going for it."
"They're really trying to kill me."
"Get out of the way idiot."
But I do not move.

I'll see the knife and still take it.
I'll see the bus and still walk into traffic,
knowing exactly how it will feel as it smashes into my frame,
dragging me along the pavement.

The street could use a little color anyway.

If Anyone Can Hide It, It's Me

Changing? But I Am!

I'm unrecognizable,
I'm full of smiles.
I've got the same problems I make the same mistakes.
Just now they have new party hats and different names.

I'll tug on a reason to be here,
a reason to be happy,
a reason that I'm thankful isn't you.

Even if the names are different,
I'll still play along.
I better get over it.
I better start enjoying this.
Just like all my problems,
I'll get dressed for the party too.

I feel great!

If Anyone Can Hide It, It's Me

Artificial Limbs

You know,
I used to think about how much comfort you gave me.
Your arms around me.
Lovingly.

Isn't it interesting how easily limbs can be replaced?
Isn't it interesting how drastically things can change?
How sympathy can be expressed by the muscles in your face.

It's comforting now,
to know how far away your arms are from me.

If Anyone Can Hide It, It's Me

Pet Plants

I'd like to think there is a reason to why I feel the way I do.
A reason why it feels like I'm always drowning.
Besides the asthma.

I feel like an overwatered plant.
My owner is careless.

When you pluck me from the ground,
and cut my roots,
 and give me away,
I hope to feel a bit at ease.

It's hard to bloom in this shade.

If Anyone Can Hide It, It's Me

The Visualization of You Murdering Me (Death Rattle)

You know I'll be smug about it,
tell you there are no flattering angles.
I can see you mouth my last words,
it's something about being strangled.

And asking if that's the best you can do?
If your grip could be tighter,
that your hands around my neck,
have always made me feel lighter.
Especially this time around,
while they're attempting to weigh me down.

My death rattle is going to sound like **"I love you."**
But I promise I don't mean it.

If Anyone Can Hide It, It's Me

Out the Door

How did you get so unlocked?
Was it easy,
or did you have to give up a lot?

Your emotions come so effortlessly.
Where are mine going?

Out the door.

If Anyone Can Hide It, It's Me

A Letter to Everything Symmetrical (And Everything I Personally Hate)

I am an advocate of asymmetry.
Just look at my face.
Look at my fucking face,
and I hope it makes you uncomfortable.

I'll spill out onto the floor,
and in a panic, everyone will run away.
I'm so happy that none of the pieces match.
It's all different shapes that were never meant to be together.
Yet here I am,
so happy.

The stain I left on your floor,
is the only accurate representation of me in my own life.
I am here to rebel.

Beauty,
I'll be at your birthday party,
looking amazing,
and yes I've been working out.

Beauty,
I'm going to spit in your face when you blow out the candles,
and you're going to thank me.

If Anyone Can Hide It, It's Me

The Consequences Catching Up to Your Actions

It's surreal,
and it's smashing against my head like a bat.
A bat wielded by an overworked salaryman,
who played college baseball.
Who's had his suspicions.
Who's just discovered me in bed with his wife.
Who still has a great swing, trust me.
My blood is going to be a sour reminder,
of their failed marriage,
stained on these expensive white sheets.

Now the moon has broken in half,
and I have not learned my lesson.
Pieces are finally falling down to greet the Earth.

And all I can do is bark at it,
tail wagging.

Growth

I've only been able to survive off the corpses of my past selves.
Everything is death and rebirth.

I'll stomp on and crush my own head,
desperate,
arms stretched outward,
reaching for whatever will touch me back.
Reaching for an answer.

There is a funeral every day that no one attends except for me.

No one mourns except for me.

If Anyone Can Hide It, It's Me

Cleft Lip and Palate

I'm starting to like the fact,
that I look like two different people,
depending on the angle you look at me.

It matches the way I feel,
like two different people.

I'm continuously content.
I'm delightfully divided,
an open wound being tended.

I may be in half but both halves are mine.

Sitcom Worthy

I'm imagining you,
sitting at the bar chewing cashews.
Sipping overpriced beers that are locally brewed.
Hopping on the hops buzz grinning in a circle of your select few.
Why not indulge?
What else is there to do?

You owe it to yourself,
just a little weekly reward,
excitingly enjoying the exquisite spoils of war.
A painted picture of the exact exponent,
for keeping one foot in the door.

Feeling tipsy,
You're making the rejection of change look easy,
keeping everyone's attention,
with a joke where the punchline went missing.
You're trying to be happy,
even when you know no one's really listening.

If Anyone Can Hide It, It's Me

Grand Finale of The Phoenix

I'm mostly about self-discovery through self-destruction.
It's probably just my ego though,
getting me fixated on the 'self' part.

You really should just focus on discovery and destruction.

What am I going to finally learn,
when I've burnt to a crisp,
by a fire I set myself?

Let's find out.

For a Moment Free

The fire in my heart has shifted to my tongue,
angry.
It's finally gone,
and I can speak again.
Pieces of you remain but they do not fester,
they are a part of me now.

No one is bothered by the flames in me.
Everyone is fine with my house burning down.
So, consider me extinguished,
I let them go,
let everything go.

I'll let you go.

Your Personal Bonfire

I've been on fire for the last year,
seems like something's finally coming out of the ashes.

I was worried there for a second,
I thought you'd never leave.
I thought you'd never put down the gasoline.

If Anyone Can Hide It, It's Me

Body Parts

You could ask some parts of my body what they think,
most will say indecision others dismay.

If my feet can keep walking without complaining,
so can I.

I am a collection of conflict,
always arguing,
nothing in my body agrees on anything.

Except to keep moving.

Minimalist

It's funny how easily I can let most things go.
Nothing is permanent,
and not many things seem worth holding on to.

Like how your name can spill out of me with such ease.
Like how I'll hand out my past and feelings with a 'thank you'
and a 'please'.

I'm overflowing,
a glass of water,
but the water doesn't know where it's going.

I've worn this shirt for three years,
just because you liked the way it looked on me.

I took it off and gave it away.

If Anyone Can Hide It, It's Me

You Can Go but My Blood Stays

I will scream until I'm blue in the face.
Until awful bits of me break and fall away.
Until my protective shell begins to rip and peel.
Until it blends with my inherited yellow,
and I look as green as I feel.

Indolence has smothered me,
leeching onto my back.
Now I will wring it by the neck,
and rip out its dozens of roots.
I've spent enough time mending my dozens of wounds.

I am finally here.

Nothing that has happened to me can hurt me as much as I can.
No one can hurt me as much as I can.
Nobody can remove the blood from my head but me.

Not even you.

If Anyone Can Hide It, It's Me

Death and Rebirth

Emptying yourself into a garden,
you're covered in soil.
The plants can't get enough.
They aren't interested in your problems,
or your ambition,
or your distress.
Just your blood and what it can do for them.

But your skin will sprout leaves,
small little stems.
Rising to the sunlight,
like they're demanding to feel its warmth.

This will be the first time you'll feel alive.

If Anyone Can Hide It, It's Me

Neither of You are Worth the Time
(But Then Again Neither Am I)

To Her:
You should have left me sooner,
or I should have left you sooner.
You were just being human.
I took everything personally,
I forgive you.

To Him:
We're similar in what we say and especially in what we've done.
It's not worth it to hold on to this hostility,
You just wanted to be happy,
who am I to ask you not to?
I forgive you.

Neither of you are worth this animosity,
neither of you are worth destroying myself.

You were just being human.

If Anyone Can Hide It, It's Me

The Icing on Top

Everyone's got a lot to say about me,
like they're thinking with my brain,
like they're where I am emotionally.
Wow, I'm so glad they understand.

Although,
I thought that I was going through a lot,
but you make me sound easy.
Like a piece of cake,
untouched,
still in the bakery.
You know I'm not as sweet as I'd like to be.

Something you're not understanding,
is every day's a wave I'm riding.
One day I'm healing,
and ripping something out.
The next I've swallowed the poison myself.
A cycle everlasting.

What I've discovered is that I'm full of a constant trauma,
and I will continue to learn to cope.
There's only one way to go and that's up.
Piece of cake.

If Anyone Can Hide It, It's Me

Continue?

If I'm speaking honestly,
I'm always chasing irony,
like it's fleeing frantically,
having stolen all my money.
It's what I'm known to do.
I'm far from full of modesty,
particularly,
when I'm drinking at two in the afternoon.

In a way this is self-help,
but really just consider it helping myself.

This is what's written in Korean,
in the fine print of my existence,
a purée of pure insolence.

And I can safely say I do not want to die,
even if my skin is so tough it aches,
I'll continue to give more than I take.
I'll continue to root in burnt soil,
sprouting malnourished stems in this black oil.

I'll continue.

If Anyone Can Hide It, It's Me

Trick Question

What am I if not a trick question?
The cause of someone else's indigestion?
A knife that cuts through lovers tension?
I'll admit I'm all the wrong answers,
to what you're asking.

But there's still an answer.
I guess that's the point.
That there's still something here,
even if no one asked.

I'm going to be here even if no one asked.

Temple

I'm doing better in so many ways,
and much worse in others.
I feel fantastic,
fantastically smothered.

This body is a constant struggle,
and I've never been comfortable,
with it being anyone's temple.

Let alone my own.

If Anyone Can Hide It, It's Me

The Tortoise

I'm rough and dry,
in a world full of water,
everything seems to reject me.

Unsightly,
like leather,
entirely.

Do you think the tortoise carrying us around ever gets tired?
I'm waiting for the day it shakes us off.

When I'm floating in the abyss of forever,
I hope I can see its face with an expression of relief.

I'll probably share that same expression too.

Diseased

I guess I just have to stop.
I keep considering myself diseased,
or rotting on the inside.

Considering myself contagious.

Something nice is trying to grow here,
I just have to let it.

If Anyone Can Hide It, It's Me

Lanterns

I'm going to strike the match.
Spit out the coal that I've been saving,
and make a bonfire out of what I don't need anymore.

It's going to keep me warm,
as I dance around the burning past.

And my face will be a lantern,
smiling bright.

If Anyone Can Hide It, It's Me

    I mentioned earlier my theory about what went wrong and why. You know, the possibility is always there that I'm stuck in a delusion so deep I can't see it. That I'm wrong. It could be me. It could have been me all along, and I'm a terrible person glazing over my mistakes by making up excuses. At this point though it doesn't matter. At this the point the past remains the past and nothing was happening to me, it was just happening. I am trying to change for the better. I recognize toxic behavior in myself and others. I am trying to improve. I want to be more, and if you've ever known me, you'll know I've never wanted anything for myself. So, this is a big deal.
    A lot of my behavior had been protection. It was habits I picked up as a child to protect myself. When you've gone through awful things during childhood you put up walls, you manifest mental blocks throughout your brain. I can barely remember anything in my childhood. I was too caught up in protective habits that I couldn't form healthy relationships. All the collective variables made me rely on her. It made me focus on her instead of my own issues. Most of my choices in life have been to avoid my own issues. Something everyone does but not everyone is completely aware of or wants to admit. That avoidance was normalized and I'm stopping that now. The more I try and retrace myself, the more I am able to view certain events in my life as more impactful than I previously had. So impactful that a lot of my behavior that protected myself as a kid became harmful. I never understood that. The fact that I do now shows how far my growth has come.
    Growth! That's the thing. That's what it's all been about. Hot damn does change get under a lot of people's skin. Most people aren't too keen on it, it's scary to them. It's still scary to me!! I've been talking a lot about myself throughout the process

If Anyone Can Hide It, It's Me

of this book, and about my own changes. My experiences good and bad leading up to how I am now. I bet you're tired of hearing me whine. I haven't talked about her growth, as I couldn't begin to comprehend it.

She was in the right to focus on herself, and I was a big human shaped roadblock. Construction ahead. I was limiting her growth. She couldn't be anything more than what she was while with me. Realizing that, I can't be as angry as I want to be, and that's a good thing. I was angry for way too long. I must learn from what I was and become someone healthier. Someone who can build themselves into the best version they can be. Relationships exist to help us figure out what we want and what we need. You are not born knowing anything, what happens to us helps us figure it out. Everyone is learning how to be a person, and for us, it got to a point where we stopped learning anything. I think back and wish I had been strong enough to let go. Strong enough to allow myself to grow and change on my own and not let myself be caught up in our relationship.

It doesn't matter if I got hurt or if I went a little crazy. What matters is how I react and how I heal. Everything I did and how I felt had more to do with me than her. How I reacted to the pain was me, and there's no shame in doing what I needed to do to cope. Every day is about growth. I've come to understand that it isn't her fault that I wasn't a part of hers. All that she did was part of the cycle that she needed to go through. Everyone has a right to do what they need to do. We all learn things differently.

I spent a lot of time cocooned. I was looking to turn into Mothman. and go fixate on a new source of light. I spent a lot of time analyzing. Repeating things like **"Her growth is her growth and mine is mine."** I'm not upset anymore over what happened or having to see her occasionally at a bar. I'm not

If Anyone Can Hide It, It's Me

sending any ill will, I may let a few not so nice words slip out from time to time, but that's just me. My whole existence could be summed up in a few not so nice words and I'm proud of that. I'm proud of myself for letting go. I've been known to hold a grudge for years. It's time I understand that holding the grudge hurts only myself. I'm trying to be my own light. I'm deciding to be.

Are you focused on yourself? We go in and out of phases where we are and aren't. Do you think you could have ever been the construction site holding someone else back? It is something we've all been at some point, some more than once. Some more than twice. I was a city-wide disaster. I'm still a wreck most days.

Don't forget to look at the other person. Don't forget that maybe what you've been giving them to help their growth has run its course and it's time to let go. I know it's never that easy though. I can tell you to consider the growth of others but that's only telling you to do something. It's up to you if you're going to do it or not. It's up to you to learn the lesson, no amount of advice will make you truly know something.

I'm going to continue to sit back and look at every angle, even the bad ones. I'm going to continue to work on myself. What matters is what I do now. What matters is what you do now. If you've been in a bad place or you're coping with trauma, how you react is going to shape you. How we respond to the pain is what defines us. Just remember that we are all a constant process. You can be more every day. Despite feeling otherwise, you can love yourself. It won't be easy cause nothing ever is, but you can do it. Every day I struggle with myself, the self-loathing and feeling drained. The feeling of being unable to do anything, or just feeling trapped. My brain needing chemicals and me

If Anyone Can Hide It, It's Me

trying to give them to it. No one can be positive all the time, but I am trying to continue to have a mindset that endures and evolves. Once you actively make the choice to put the energy into something it becomes a reality. So, exclaim today, face red and breathing hard, that you will be more and that you will grow. You will love yourself! If anyone can do it, it's you!

Nothing in life happens to you, it just happens. You don't get thrown out into existence with anything promised to you either. It's hard to get passed that little, or large, ego in your head that says otherwise. When someone stops loving you, it hurts but they are their own person. What a strange concept right? Seems like I should have been able to grasp it without all the pain, but you know, can't see the logical forest through the emotional trees. We can complain but the world doesn't spin for us. Gravity doesn't pull you down because it's worried, you'll go flying. Earth has no opinion of you.

Everyone is just trying to get their shit together. Everyone is complex and complicated and there is never really a right answer. We are all on this planet attending a party that no one threw for anyone and we really did not want to come in the first place. We are all awkwardly moving around trying to make the best of it, trying to find the one dog or cat at the party so we don't have to talk to anyone. We all want to lay down and pretend none of this is happening, but we can't. So, enjoy the party. Life is going to continue to happen, feelings will get hurt but there is no force making it happen to you specifically. The universe is not out to get you no matter how much it feels like it.

You're made up of every experience you've ever had. It's all material building your wonderful self. Every little thing makes up a different part of you. So, put yourself fully into what you do every day. Understand that there is only so much life to

If Anyone Can Hide It, It's Me

live and you should be striving every day to improve and be better than yesterday self. Find passion in something and put everything you have into it. Half-assing all the time is terrible, don't you think? Start doing things for you. Start doing things that you know are good for you, because at the end of the day you're stuck with yourself. You might as well make your own company enjoyable. You might as well be full-assing things!

    Believe me I get it. If anyone can hide it, it's you, but you shouldn't have to. Let it out, all the things you've been keeping under the surface. If you feel like you're stuck just know that it's not permanent. The way you feel now, the people you're with, what you feel like you must hide, could completely change in a month or a year. Just like the planet that we grudgingly stand on, we are going to keep spinning. If you're feeling dizzy, don't worry. We all do at times. Every time my world ended, the next day still happened and I eventually felt just fine again. Every emotional blow made me stronger, it made me grow more. The only thing that's permanent is what you learn from it all. I was stuck in a cycle and it took a lot of self-analysis to break out of it. I've learned a lot but I'm still growing. We are all still growing.

If Anyone Can Hide It, It's Me

You've reached the end! Good thing too, I bet I was getting kind of annoying there, huh? If I was a better writer maybe I could have included a couple of those *Choose Your Own Adventure* pages and you could have got to the good and bad endings. Good ending being that you get to put the book down maybe have yourself a coffee. Bad ending being you're eaten by a werewolf? I guess I'm not that imaginative!

I'd like to thank everyone who supported me during the harder times of the last couple of years, I wouldn't be who I am without you! I'd also like to thank anyone who decided to pick this book up and read it. Because I never thought it would be a reality. I'm someone who kind of grew up never really wanting anything for himself. I'm sure I covered that in the book somewhere. So, this means a lot to me that I actively put my writing out there and wanted to create. It's been an attempt to connect and evolve. I'm sure you're tired of hearing all about that.

I want you to take something away from this. If you've had bad experiences or if you've been hurt, I want you to try as much as you can to become better from it. It is so easy to dive down inside yourself and come out bitter and angry. I want you to be more aware of yourself. I want you to figure out what's been eating you and why. Love is the answer to everything. Not just romantic love, but all love. Love, empathy and understanding. Acceptance and vulnerability. As you've reached the end of this book, I want you to think about what that means to you.

Sayonara, c'est la vie. Whatever happens, happens, baby!

If Anyone Can Hide It, It's Me

Photo by @truecalidad

Matthew Stegman,

26, has been writing since he was a sophomore in high school. He has no notable accomplishments, but he makes up for it in charisma. Throughout his life Matthew has always had a passion for literature and art. The Altruistic Hedonist, The Uneducated Prick, he strives every day to be a little better than the last. Living in Florida, he continues to write and work on his many creative projects.

Made in the USA
Columbia, SC
15 May 2025

57883195R00105